JIM SHORE ANGEL

COLORING BOOK

INCLUDES 3D DETAILS

Fons&Porter

CINCINNATI, OHIO

A Note from Jim

Some people call my studio controlled chaos. I confess that's probably true, except for the controlled part. I like to have a lot going on. At any given moment I can have a dozen or so projects in the works, everything from bronze casting to stonecutting to glass molding, with characters ranging from Santa Claus to Abraham Lincoln to Tinker Bell. All that activity creates its own sort of energy, a combination of elements and design with multiple levels of discovery I find stimulating. I love the complexity and variation, the constant sense of movement. It's a perfect environment for me, and in some ways it has mirrored in my art.

There's only one constant in all that commotion. No matter what else I have going on, whether I have five projects in the hopper or 20, I'm always working on an angel. Angels are a staple in my art; over the years, I've created thousands. It's a subject I love, an image that keeps inspiring, and an emotional touchstone I can use a lot of different ways. Sometimes they have a specific meaning or sentiment, celebrating love or courage or the bonds between family and friends. Sometimes they commemorate a special occasion or holiday, the connection we feel at the heart of Easter, Thanksgiving and, of course, Christmas. Often they're just an expression of the wonder I find in the world around me, the magic of a garden or the beauty of a butterfly's wings. Each one has a special meaning to me; they're an insight into what I was thinking and feeling at specific moments. This book is a collection of my favorites. I think as you go through it you'll be able to see why.

I don't mind saying my angels reflect the beauty and love shown me by the women in my life. With my wife Jan, our five daughters and half-dozen granddaughters, I've been incredibly blessed. This book was actually Jan's brainchild, a new way to share my art and creative process. We worked on it together, and, as in so many things in my life, it's better because of her. It was Jan's idea to add the special pages with the three-dimensional elements. It's a simple, but brilliant way to enhance your fun. Just color and cut out the elements on the 3D details pages and use dimensional crafting tape to attach your cut-out over the original design. My favorite is probably the Lion and Lamb design, which has some real scale to it! The result is a sculpted, three-dimensional effect, which I think adds a lot to the finished work. Try it; I think you'll be amazed! Whatever your approach—coloring, cutting or crafting how you see fit—I hope you enjoy this book as much as we enjoyed putting it together. It has been a real labor of love for Jan and me, with angel designs close to my heart, from my family to yours.

Jim Shore

The Joy of Christmas Morn

a content + ecommerce company

19   18   17   16   5   4   3   2   1

Distributed in Canada by Fraser Direct
100 Armstrong Avenue
Georgetown, ON, Canada L7G 5S4
Tel: (905) 877-4411

Distributed in the U.K. and Europe by F&W MEDIA INTERNATIONAL
Brunel House, Newton Abbot, Devon, TQ12 4PU, England
Tel: (+44) 1626 323200, Fax: (+44) 1626 323319
E-mail: enquiries@fwmedia.com

SRN: R2489
ISBN-13: 978-1-4402-4734-7

Edited by Amelia Johanson
Cover design by Erin Alexander
Production coordinated by Bryan Davidson
Illustrations by Jim Shore

p. 37

p. 17

p. 7

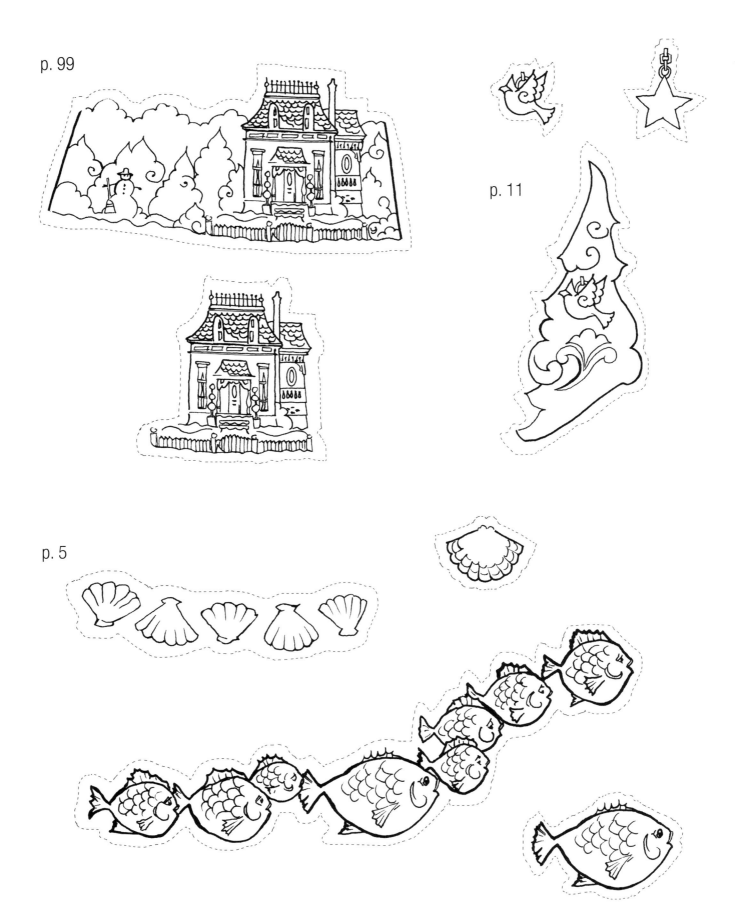

p. 99

p. 11

p. 5

p. 91

p. 19

p. 33

p. 99

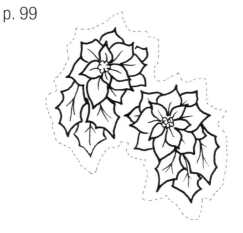